"Up to now, you have refuted everything which has been said. You have done nothing to point out the true Dharma to us."

-A student reproaching Huang Po, from the Blofeld's *Zen Teaching of Huang Po*

- To pursue a single Dharma is not Zen, which embraces many/all paths of attainment.

Not Zen

To all the followers of the Way;
Especially those lunatics @reddit's /r/Zen,
without whom I would have spent more time drinking tea.

-ewk

I am in no way qualified to write this book.

Anyone who implies that they are qualified to say anything about Zen, qualified by having a teacher, by a lineage, by years of study, by a title or a certificate… all of these are not Zen. It is one thing to talk about the history of the conversation and who said what, it is error to say "Zen is".

I would also encourage skepticism with regard to anyone who wears a robe and shaves their head. This is not normal behavior, and Zen Masters have been skeptical of these sorts of people since one of them crossed the sea to China 1500 years ago.

If anyone takes offense at any of this, that is of course not Zen.

Note to the Reader:

I don't reference many books. If you want to know about Zen, go to the source. Anybody can put "Zen" in the title of their book. Most of those who put "Zen" in their titles in the U.S. are Buddhists who call themselves Zen Buddhists. When you read the old Zen Masters you will see that they don't talk like the Buddhists who say "Zen", they do not teach like the Buddhists who say "Zen".

Since I'm keeping the bibliography rather short I'm sure some will say that my parroting of these old men is necessarily incomplete, but this is silly. In this tradition of Zen the old men all repeat each other, mostly without attribution. It is almost as if they expect that everyone has heard it all before. If you read Mumonkan or Huang Po or Joshu (or Tung Shan) and then turn to Mumonkan or Huang Po or Joshu (or Tung Shan) for contrast you will find none. These old men all say the same thing. When someone claims they are in this lineage of old men and says something new, then make your bow and depart.

The famous religious leader Dogen said something new, as do the others in the Dogen Buddhism crowd. Huang Po said that those believing in the Buddha's words were not Zen, this is true of those believing in anybody's words. When you follow the authority of a particular teacher, this is called "faith" and it is the beginning of religion. Religion is not Zen.

You can certainly try to put your faith in the old men of the Zen lineage, but where does that lead you?

Ummon said, "The real Emptiness does not destroy things; the real Emptiness is not different from materiality."

Then a monk asked him, "What is the real Emptiness?"

Ummon said, "Do you hear the sound of a bell?"

"That's the sound of a bell," said the monk.

"Even when you have reached the year of the Donkey, will you still be dreaming?" asked Ummon.

Contents

A monk asked, "How can you not slander the ancients and be faithful to them at the same time?"

Joshu said, "What are you doing?"

Introduction

Disclaimer: There is no such thing as an introduction to Zen.

All over the world teachers claim to teach Zen. All over the world students claim to be practicing Zen. All of this teaching and all of this practicing is mostly just Buddhism that uses the word Zen to attract followers or somewhere back in the history of that particular religion was someone who took the word to attract followers. It is also possible that there was some sort of a misunderstanding at some point, and to this day nobody in this sort of Buddhism bothered to read anything.

If you read any book by any of the Zen Masters that followed Bodhidharma's Way you will of course understand this for yourself immediately. The majority of people who teach Zen or practice it do not hold themselves to what was written about Zen since Bodhidharma. They believe what they are told, they recline on their faith, they worship the authority of their teachers, they invent as they go along. There is nothing wrong with this, but why call it Zen? The old men that the word "Zen" refers to did not practice any religion, they did not teach any doctrine or dogma or technique, they did not enlighten anyone, and they did not leave any particular path to be followed.

If you are one of these who claim to receive a package that was never sent to you, those who are content with religion, then call yourselves Buddhists, or Dogen Buddhists, and be on your way. Leave the Zen of the old men alone, it is not a medicine to be taken lightly, it is not a Gate to be sought out by those who desire peace or compassion, comfort or healing. As was said by one of these old men a long time ago, **"The Buddha is like stretching out the hand, the Way is like clenching the fist.**"[1] He wasn't kidding.

This book is not really revolutionary, despite my use of the word in the title at the insistence of my imaginary publisher. As I have said, as I will continue to show here, anyone who picks up a book of conversations of the old Masters will immediately see the revolution is not mine, it is theirs.

Their Zen was revolutionary, and given all the meditation and all the teaching of dogma and all the faith-based-Buddhisms pretending to be Zen, it still is.

---

[1] p21 "Zen and Zen Classics, Volume 3 - Reginald Horace Blyth - Google Books."
<http://books.google.com/books/about/Zen_and_Zen_classics.html?id=sgQYA AAAIAAJ>

Warning

As I said, this *not Zen* revolution is the Masters' revolution. Bodhidharma began it with his "no merit" and it was continued on after him. Zen Masters teach revolution against every teacher, every teaching, every belief, every idea, every thought... revolution against even Zen Masters themselves.

If you meet someone on the way who does not preach revolution, who does not live revolution against every teacher and every teaching, then they are not Zen. If you meet someone who wears special clothes or has special ceremonies or knows a special method of sitting, they are not Zen. Nod to them, and pass by in your search for *the Way*.

You will find many quotes from Zen Masters in this book. I bolded them for you. I did this not because these old men are any kind of authority (like Dogen or the Bible) rather because these old men are describing something which is likely not what you have been taught or told or made to practice. What they are describing, or *pointing to*, was since a long time ago called Zen. Over the last few hundred years, this name has been misused by various people in error.

There are other books with Zen in the title that do not begin with these old men and end with these old men and go only as far as these old men pointed. This is a symptom of "not Zen." Not because the old men were teaching a particular truth, but because they taught no particular truth, and this was called "Zen." When someone *teaches* you, ask yourself: Is this the Zen of those old men? Or does a teacher take the word "Zen" but leave the old men behind? There is Zen without the old men, but it leaves everything else behind as well.

A monk asked, "I have come a long way, please instruct me."

Joshu said, "You have only just entered my door. Is it proper that I spit in your face?"

1. Proper/improper are not Zen, nor is the distance traveled relevant to this thinky.

2. The teachings are by nature like a slap/spit in the face.

1. Fundamental concepts of Zen

It will become clear as we wander through this book that there is very little, if anything, that Zen Masters said about Zen. Some people who call themselves Zen Buddhists will of course tell you all about their ideas and claim that these ideas they create are Zen, but these sorts of ideas require authorities, faith and practices.

Since Bodhidharma, the First Patriarch of Zen, arrived in China, there has been no "is" in Zen. Anyone who begins by saying, "Zen is..." has lost the Way. Once any of us takes the step of trying to intellectualize Zen with "is" then whatever follows is not Zen.

There is, unsurprisingly for some of us, a great deal which can be said about what is not Zen. When Bodhidharma arrived in China, the story goes, he was invited to meet the Emperor of China. The Emperor asked Bodhidharma how much merit was earned by building temples and copying sacred texts. Bodhidharma said, "None whatever" or something like it in Chinese, and thus the first "not Zen" was uttered. The Emperor asked, "What is the essence of Buddhism?" and Bodhidharma replied, "Void, and nothing holy therein." Thus, the second not Zen was uttered.

Everything you think! Void. Everything you value! Not Zen.

Then the Emperor asked, "Who am I talking to?" Bodhidharma replied with something in Chinese like, "No idea." See? Perhaps the Emperor thinks to trap Bodhidharma by identifying a voice of authority, but Bodhidharma says, "not Zen." There is no voice of authority in Zen. From these more or less unimpressive exchanges the entire lineage of Zen is born, a lineage of Questions and Answers, a lineage of skeptical and annoying students, a lineage of even more irritating, vague, and disinterested Masters, a lineage of revolution against institutionalized beliefs and rote answers, against wisdom and compassion, against teachings and all that.

Nowadays Zen is rather uncommon despite the wide use of the word by a great many well-meaning religious people who know a great deal about their faiths and beliefs but nonetheless have no Zen.

While I haven't read everything, it is interesting to note that both Huang Po and Joshu, two of the Masters who will walk along with us in this not Zen conversation, single out Bodhidharma as the beginning of the Zen lineage. These Masters do not point to Buddha.

"From the days when Bodhidharma first transmitted naught but the One Mind, there has been no other valid Dharma."[2] - Huang Po

This sort of talk is confusing to people who think of Zen as Zen Buddhism. Zen is no more Zen Buddhism than it is Zen Bodhidharma-ism.

The briefest history ever: The old men lineage of Zen

There were six Zen Patriarchs in China, and the Sixth Patriarch ended the tradition of Patriarchy. There is little historical evidence supporting the "Indian lineage" that links Bodhidharma's teachers to the Buddha himself. People will tell you that there was Zen in India of course, and they believe it. But this Indian lineage

---

[2]"The Zen Teaching of Huang-Po: On the Transmission of Mind: John ..."
<http://www.amazon.com/Zen-Teaching-Huang-Po-Transmission-Mind/dp/0802150926>

of Zen is faith-based, not historical. Some Masters refer to this lineage, like Ummon, who uses it as part of a fairytale.

There is little historical evidence for the "Buddha Flower" koan where Buddha transmits Zen by holding up a flower. Does this matter at all to Zen? All the lineages and the koans are just stories. There is no reason to believe (in) any of them or take them any more seriously than a runny nose. Some Masters refer to this koan, so clearly what is true is irrelevant to whatever it is that Zen Masters point to.

After the last Patriarch, there followed a succession of Masters that, along with the Patriarchs, I refer to as the old men. These old men are not anything more than old men, and when I say "one of the old men says," I mean, "Are you talking about what they were talking about, or are you talking about your faith/practice/religion?" The only authority in these old men is their reporting of what they said, that they said it, and that they didn't say something else. That they said anything doesn't make it true.

Nearer the end of a particularly popular period for Zen was a Master named Mumon. He compiled a very short list of Cases, or koans, which are basically fragments of conversations with Zen Masters. Mumon also wrote a brief comment on each Case as instruction to the novices. As added instruction Mumon also wrote a short poem about each Case. Throughout the history of Zen there seems to have been a great many Masters who liked to compose verses. Mumon was something of a comedian, so there is no reason to take any of what he says seriously even though he was one of the (in)famous Masters.

There is a particularly inspiring map of the Zen lineage from Ferguson's Zen Chinese Heritage over at

Southmountaintours.com[3] Of course this is not authoritative. Who knows if any of them were Masters? For every Zen Master there have been, there are, ten thousand people who use the title and *believe, out of faith,* they know what it means.

Mumon's book is called Mumonkan, and it is a delightful collection of nonsense. Any discussion of Zen that doesn't include at least one Master from the Mumonkan is likely not a discussion about Zen but a discussion about the Buddhist religion. Generally those who start with Mumonkan's Masters and Bodhidharma are talking about Zen and those that start with Buddha or Dogen or Zazen sitting meditation can be broadly described as belonging to the religions of Buddhism, not only because of what they claim, but also because of how they claim it.

The Four Statements of Zen

At some point several one liners from various sources were compiled into a starting point, a sort of introduction, to Zen conversations. These so called "Four Statements of Zen" are not authoritative, they are more like a greeting card version of a koan. Nevertheless there are a great many people who think they are studying Zen but have never heard of these Four Statements, and even more tellingly, these people would not agree at all that these Four Statements summarize what they are studying. This is one clue that someone is not studying Zen at all, but one of the Buddhisms.

---

[3] "Map Zen Ancestors - South Mountain China Tours."
<http://www.southmountaintours.com/images/Zen_ancestor_map/AM150306.pdf>

Here are the Four Statements of Zen as translated by D.T. Suzuki:

1 **A special transmission outside the Scriptures,**
2 **Not depending upon the letter,**
3 **But pointing directly to the Mind; and**
4 **Leading us to see the Nature itself, thereby making us attain Buddhahood.**

*An aphorism defying absolutes ※ with regards to the world.

There are different translations, and all of them are interesting in their own way. For example, "not depending on words and sentences" is a different interpretation of the second line.

When D.T. Suzuki says "the Nature itself" some have translated this as Self-Nature, or True Nature. Seeing yourself clearly is the idea, not seeing the self when it is doing something like studying scriptures, not seeing the self when you are doing something like pretending to be "not doing" something like meditation. Not seeing the self in terms of past or future or dreams or interests or desires or opinions. We are speaking of the self before your parents were born. That self.

Sometimes the fourth statement that ends with "attain Buddhahood" is translated as "A freedom arising from seeing into the self-nature" but I forget where I read that. The problem for most of us is that there is no agreement about what a Buddha is among the many Buddhisms, and of course no one will say among the old men.

What the old men said

What follows is a taste of the Zen we are talking about here. If none of these are familiar to you, welcome to Zen! Zen is not whatever it is that you have been taught about. Sometimes these old men called Zen by other names. Sometimes they talk about it as the Way (there are a thousand paths, but only one Way) sometimes they talked about it as the only real Dharma (there isn't one) sometimes they talked about it as the real Buddhism, free of any teaching and beyond any sort of idea. Zen Masters use Taoist language and Buddhist language because it was the context of the culture.

This Zen conversation began long before Dogen taught Zazen meditation, long after Buddha, long before Western Buddhism, just about where Bodhidharma spoke to the Emperor. Mumon was a Zen Master who, rather unusually, wrote about Zen. Mumon said this about it:

> **"For the practical study of Zen, you must pass the barriers set up by the masters of Zen. The attainment of this mysterious illumination means cutting off the workings of the ordinary mind completely. If you have not done this and passed the barrier, you are a phantom among the undergrowth and weeds. Now what is this barrier? It is simply "[No]", the Barrier of the Gate of Zen and this is why it is called 'The Gateless Barrier of the Zen Sect."[4]**

If you have not heard of Mumon's book, Mumonkan, if you are unfamiliar with the title "The Gateless Gate", is it any wonder that you believe anything you are told about Zen? Without these old men to guide you, you are just a sheep of ignorance wandering

---

[4] p31 "Zen and Zen Classics, Volume 4 - Mumonkan: RH Blyth - Amazon.com." <http://www.amazon.com/Zen-Classics-Volume-Mumonkan/dp/B000OF55KQ>

around among wolves who know things. Ha! The old men will give you some medicine for this knowing sickness.

Astute students will no doubt notice that I did not faithfully reproduce Blyth's quote in the paragraph above, instead translating Mu as No. A conversation about Mu will likely require a special section of its own on account of all the Mu worshipping that goes on here in the West. Blyth was a Zen scholar who lived in Japan before the Second World War. While Blyth was not a Zen Master he had a particular fondness for them. He collected many quotes from them in his four volume series titled Zen and Zen Classics.

> **So those who seek the Way must enter it with the suddenness of a knife-thrust.**[5] - Huang Po

Zen is sometimes referred to as the Sudden School of Buddhism, because Zen enlightenment is not something achieved through study or practice. Many religions have enlightenments that are a particular attainment or experience, but these are not Zen.

> **Goso said, "When you meet a man of the Way on the way, do not greet him with words; do not greet him with silence; tell me, how will you greet him?"**[6]

> Case 36, Mumonkan

---

[5] p111"The Zen Teaching of Huang-Po: On the Transmission of Mind: John ..." <http://www.amazon.com/Zen-Teaching-Huang-Po-Transmission-Mind/dp/0802150926>

[6] "Zen and Zen Classics: Mumonkan - Reginald ... - Google Books." <http://books.google.com/books/about/Zen_and_Zen_Classics_Mumonkan.html?id=B3zXAAAAMAAJ>

Sometimes I refer to this as "Zen is not speech, Zen is not silence; Speak!" If you have heard of this Zen, then you cannot help yourself. If you haven't, then no doubt this sort of injunction will confuse you.

> **When Bankei was preaching at Ryumon temple, a Shinshu priest, who believed in salvation through the repetition of the name of the Buddha of Love, wanted to debate with him.**
>
> **Bankei was in the midst of a talk when the priest appeared, but the fellow made such a disturbance that Bankei stopped his discourse and asked about the noise.**
>
> **"The founder of our sect," boasted the priest, "has such miraculous powers that he held a brush in his hand on one bank of the river, his attendant held up a paper on the other bank and the teacher wrote the holy name of Amida through the air. Can you do such a thing?"**
>
> **Bankei replied, "Perhaps your fox can perform that trick, but that is not the manner of Zen. My miracle is when I am hungry I eat, and when I am thirsty I drink."[7]**

Bankei was himself quoting another Zen Master. They are always quoting each other, such jokers! The part about it being a miracle though, that's serious. If you do not understand this miracle, likely you have been taught to think Zen is something. Now, when it turns out not to be, you find you have confused yourself. Have some tea, it will pass.

---

[7] "101 Zen Stories." <http://www.101Zenstories.com/>

13

1. Zen is not faith or acts performed as such
2. The mindful state of Zen is omnipresent when achieved.

A monk asked, "What is a person who understands matters perfectly?

Joshu said, "Obviously it is great practice."

The monk said, "It's not yet clear to me; do you practice or not?"

Joshu said, "I wear cloths and eat food."

The monk said, "Wearing clothes and eating food are ordinary things. It's still not clear to me; do you practice or not?"

Joshu said, "You tell me, what am I doing every day?"[8] ① Ever-present in nature

Many Buddhists will talk about their *practice*, which is the special or specific things they do as part of their religious exercise or observance. Even back in Joshu's day monks wanted to know about the personal habits of Zen Masters, part of their idea being that if you *do* what a Zen Master does then you can experience their enlightenment. Enlightenment doesn't come from doing anything in particular, even if you meditate and pretend that you aren't doing anything to confuse everyone. Anything you do every day that is not ordinary is practice, and there is no practice in Zen. You can't make something ordinary by pretending for long enough, but it might seem like it.

Some will argue that their "practice" has *become* what they do every day and is therefore not to be distinguished from ordinary. This is a delightful error because it assumes that very thing it is trying to prove... that *doing* can become *not doing* by doing it for long enough that you don't think about doing it. Still,

[8] #181, "The Recorded Sayings of Zen Master Joshu: James Green, Kreido ..." <http://www.amazon.com/Recorded-Sayings-Zen-Master-Joshu/dp/157062870X>

even if you don't think about it, what you *do* on your religious path is still you *doing something* for religious reasons.

The Zen master Mu-nan had only one successor. His name was Shoju. After Shoju had completed his study of Zen. Mu-nan called him into his room. 'I am getting old,' he said, 'and as far as I know Shoju, you are the only one who will carry out this teaching. Here is a book. It has been passed down from master to master for seven generations. I also have added many points according to my understanding. The book is very valuable and I am giving it to you to represent your successor ship.'

'If the book is such an important thing, you had better keep it,' Shoju replied.' I received your Zen without writing and am satisfied with it as it is.'

'I know that,' said Mu-nan. 'Even so, this work has been carried from master to master for seven generations, so you may keep it as a symbol of having received the teaching. Here.'

The two happened to be talking before a brazier. The instant Shoju felt the book in his hands he thrust it into the flaming coals. He had no lust for possessions.

Mu-nan who never had been angry before yelled: 'What are you doing?'

Shoju shouted back: 'What are you saying!'[9]

① Symbols are devoid of Zen
② Right/Wrong are also devoid, so such actions are within Zen

---

[9] "Zen Flesh, Zen Bones, Paul Reps."
<http://playpen.meraka.csir.co.za/~acdc/education/Dr_Anvind_Gupa/Learners_Library_7_March_2007/Resources/books/Zen.pdf>

Whenever there are symbols of attainment, this is not Zen. Whenever the teacher distinguishes himself from the students, this is not Zen. Often there was a place for the Master to sit when he received people. Was it a throne? Often there was a podium used by speakers to address the monks, but some Zen Masters never used it. The same robes, the same food, the same work. Zen Masters were just like everyone else. Nowadays, many Buddhists and Dogen Buddhism followers like to have certificates and badges and all the trappings of organized religions. This is not Zen. It's not a reason to hate, but it's not Zen.

> **Asked by a monk, "What is the doctrine that transcends all Buddhas and Masters?" Ummon immediately held aloft his staff, and said, "I call this a staff, what do you call it?" The monk was silent. Again Ummon held up the staff, saying, "The doctrine transcending the teachings of all the Buddhas and masters - was not that what you asked me about?" The monk was still silent.[10]**

Ummon was not to be trifled with. When he was asked a question he answered with Zen. Zen has no doctrine, no dogma. What was Ummon teaching? If anyone wants to explain it to you, slap them soundly.

① There is no dogma, if the Monk thought the staff was not a staff, it would illustrate the

---

[10] p126 "Zen and Zen Classics: Mumonkan - Reginald ... - Google Books." <http://books.google.com/books/about/Zen_and_Zen_Classics_Mumonkan.html?id=B3zXAAAAMAAJ>

A monk asked Nansen, "Is there a Dharma that no one has taught?" Nansen replied, "Yes." "What is this truth," asked the monk, "which no one has so far taught?" Nansen answered, "It is not mind; it is not Buddha, it is not things." – Mumonkan, Case 27

All the time people go to teachers and ask their questions and the teacher gives them something and the people go about their business, clutching what was given to them. Tell me, what did Nansen give the monk? *→ He told him what the lesson was not*
→ He did not embrace a single truth.

Relinquishment of everything is the Dharma, and he who understands this is a Buddha, but the relinquishment of all delusions leaves no Dharma on which to lay hold.[11] -Huang Po *→ not nihilism*

Who ever talked this way to you? Some will say this, but then teach you a dharma anyway. This is called, "mouthing the words."

If you understand the first word of Zen
You understand the last;
But these two words
Are not one word. - Mumonkan, Case 13

What if you go around asking people what the last word of Zen is? A good question! Now, make your bow and depart.

Rinzai and Fuke once went to a vegetarian banquet given in their honor by a local supporter. Rinzai presented a koan to Fuke while they were eating.

---

[11] p40 "The Zen Teaching of Huang-Po: On the Transmission of Mind: John ..." <http://www.amazon.com/Zen-Teaching-Huang-Po-Transmission-Mind/dp/0802150926>

"A hair swallows the vast ocean, a mustard seed contains Mount Sumeru. Does this happen by means of supernatural powers, or is the whole body like this?" Fuke responded to the koan by kicking over the table.

"You ruffian!" cried Rinzai.

"What place is this to speak of rough and refined?" Fuke countered.

The next day they again went out together to a supporter's luncheon, and Rinzai opened the discussion, saying, "How does today's meal compare with yesterday's?" Fuke kicked over the table again, and Rinzai said, "You certainly understand it, but you're still a ruffian." This time Fuke replied, "You blind man; what are you doing preaching roughness and fineness in the Buddha-Dharma!" Rinzai countered by sticking out his tongue, an old Chinese expression of admiration.[12]

There are a million websites that use the word Zen these days, and yet there are very few ruffians. Rinzai enjoyed lunching with Fuke, but how many others would? Mostly we have people who mouth the words and sit staring vacuously into space in search of purity or compassion or peace. They should invite me to lunch.

① Even physical interpretations of the world are implied (illusions) and defined as freely as rough/refined.

---

[12] p34 "Crazy Clouds: Zen radicals, rebels, and reformers - Perle ..." 2011. <http://books.google.com/books/about/Crazy_Clouds.html?id=LcAKAAAAYA AJ>

Interlude:

Ummon once appeared in the pulpit, and said, "In this school of Zen no words are needed; what, then, is the ultimate essence of Zen teaching?" Thus himself proposing the question, he extended both his arms, and without further remarks came down from the pulpit.

① The *operation* of thought transcends words
② Words are definitions and thus not Zen in some sense.

19

2. Buddhism is not Zen

"If you accept the Buddha-Vehicle, which is the doctrine transmitted by Bodhidharma, you will not speak of such things [as the Three Vehicles] but merely point to the One Mind which is without identity or difference, without cause and effect."[13] - Huang Po

I watched a lecture where one of the speakers, a man named John Peacock, talked about the word Buddhism[14]. Peacock is a secular Buddhist, which is only slightly more popular than being a Zen Master, although the two are in no way related (in contrast Buddhist Masters are very popular). Peacock discussed the invention of the word "Buddhism" in the early 1800's, by a travel blogger visiting the East for the first time. The blogger thought that all those who preached "the Dharma" were talking about the same "Dharma". The reality is rather different, Zen Masters never considered themselves "Buddhists" at all, explicitly rejecting other Dharmas.

This is surprisingly easy to confirm, and even more surprisingly completely unacknowledged by most Western "Buddhists." Peacock says that his reading of early "Buddhist" texts suggests that there is no common denominator that binds all of these various Eastern religious ideologies together, other than the name itself.

---

[13] p73 "The Zen Teaching of Huang-Po: On the Transmission of Mind: John ..." <http://www.amazon.com/Zen-Teaching-Huang-Po-Transmission-Mind/dp/0802150926>

[14] Uncertain Minds: How the West Misunderstands Buddhism, <https://www.youtube.com/watch?v=hXYBtT4uN30&feature>

This is the first sort of "Buddhism is not Zen". Not only is "Buddhism" an English word and a Western idea, but more to the point Zen is not a religion or a philosophy, nor is the group of religions and philosophies called "Buddhism" definite enough to make a claim on Zen beyond the use of common cultural words and ideas or geographic origins.

On a side note, there is a sort of rule of thumb I use in wandering around investigating people who use the word Zen. Those that believe in Buddha and a lineage that begins with Buddha, these I call Dogen Buddhism. Those that say their lineage begins with Bodhidharma, as Joshu and Huang Po did, these might be following some Zen Master. There was no word for "Buddhism" back in their time, but collectively many of these "Buddhists" talked about the same thing: preaching the Dharma. Those who preach the Dharmas they believe come from the Buddha will claim a lineage to Buddha. Those who preach a Dharma from Bodhidharma say their lineage begins there. Not terribly scientific, but then I do not authenticate, I irritate.

The second sort of "Buddhism is not Zen" is even vaguer. In the West there are a great many people who believe in karma, reincarnation, meditation, compassion, the eightfold path, and these sorts of ideas associated with Buddha. Zen has nothing to do with any of that. Pick up any book of sayings by an old Master and you will find the old man throwing that business out with both hands. Zen is not Buddhism.

The third sort of "Buddhism is not Zen" is the Eastern Buddhisms that call themselves Zen Buddhism, arriving here from places like Thailand and Malaysia. These Buddhisms call themselves "Zen Buddhism" (Dogen Buddhism), but there is no mention of the lineage of the old men, no reference to their teachings, no compatibility between this Dogen Buddhism and the

Zen lineage from Bodhidharma. These Dogen Buddhism teach loving compassion, not what Huang Po teaches, **"compassion really means not conceiving of sentient beings to be delivered."**[15] Many of them teach and practice meditation which is not taught as a special path by any Zen Master.

These are the general problems with associating Zen with Buddhism, but there are a few significant points that are useful in illustrating just how much the Buddhisms, in any form, are not Zen.

No good and evil in Zen

Buddhism is in one way or another concerned with preferring some kinds of intents or behavior over others. Any internet search of "Buddhism Good Evil" will produce a wide variety of perspectives on the subject in line with the argument that there isn't one Buddhism, but rather a heterogeneous mixture of Buddhisms. I will deftly sidestep this problem by focusing on the act of differentiation itself, without which notions of good and evil cannot be used, cannot in fact be imagined.

"To set up what you like against what you dislike, this is the disease of the mind"[16] - 3rd Patriarch (*aka* 3P)

Good and evil are really, at the end of the day, stuff that somebody said "I like this, I don't like that." Maybe it was God, maybe it was Buddha, maybe it was The Man, who cares? Good

---

[15] p84 "The Zen Teaching of Huang-Po: On the Transmission of Mind: John ..." <http://www.amazon.com/Zen-Teaching-Huang-Po-Transmission-Mind/dp/0802150926>

[16] "ON BELIEVING IN MIND (SHINJIN-NO-MEI) by Seng-t'san." 2004. <http://home.primusonline.com.au/peony/faith_in_mind.htm>

and evil is just another sort of differentiation. There is an old story about a farmer who had a horse that ran away. Then the horse comes back with some other horses, then the farmer's son breaks his arm trying to ride the horses, then the army comes by conscripting but won't take the son because his arm is broken. The farmer has neighbor who, at every turn of events of this horse situation, leans over the fence and says to the farmer, "Lucky!" or "Unlucky. In the blink of an eye lucky becomes unlucky, unlucky becomes lucky. When lucky and unlucky or good and evil changes in the blink of an eye, how real is it?

> "**When you see good and evil in this world, do not cling to them, nor shun them, nor be defiled by them.**"[17] - 6th Patriarch (*aka* **6P**)

Now, a contentious person might argue that 6P isn't saying "no such thing as good and evil". However, this "do not cling to them" rules out trying to do good and trying not to do evil. Trying to do them is certainly clinging, trying not to do them is certainly shunning. Zen has no such ideas as good and evil, some Buddhisms do, and those Buddhisms are not Zen.

> The [Sixth] **Patriarch said, "Do not think 'This is good! This is bad!' At such a moment, what is the Original Self of Monk Myo?"**[18] - Mumonkan, Case 23

---

[17] Platform Sutra of the Sixth Patriarch, p31 "Studies in Zen: Suzuki: 9780802216786: Amazon.com: Books." 2006.
<http://www.amazon.com/Studies-Zen-Suzuki/dp/0802216781>

[18] Case 23, "The Gateless Gate Index." <http://www.sacred-texts.com/bud/glg/index.htm>

This is a very famous exchange, a little history and a little legend, which happened when the Fifth Patriarch gave the robe and bowl, the symbols of Patriarch-ness, to the successor he chose, the Sixth Patriarch. The Fifth, the story goes, picked the Sixth because of a poetry contest. True story. The Fifth was concerned that people, and by people I mean bald, robe wearing people, would not accept the Sixth because he was an outsider (probably also annoying) so the Fifth gave the Sixth the robe and bowl in secret and told him to take a little trip out of town. The monk who expected to be Sixth but was passed over gives chase and catches the Sixth in the mountains. The Sixth puts the robe and bowl down on a rock, and as the story goes, tells the monk to take them, but the monk can't pick them up. Instead, the monk asks the Sixth for instruction, and this is what the Sixth says to him... DO NOT THINK AT SUCH A MOMENT... (a nice piece of not Zen by the way). This is just a story, the monk that chased the 6P, monk Myo, is known historically as the head monk of the Northern School. The Northern School was certainly Buddhist, not Zen.

Look at all the Buddhisms, telling you what to value, what to think in terms of how to see the world. Some of these Buddhisms will say that this sort of instruction is just for novices, but then they will tell you to follow it anyway. But in Zen there are only those that don't know what to follow. Nothing else. What I mean is there is only one teaching in Zen. **"Saying that**

there is no Dharma to be explained in words is called preaching the Dharma."[19]

On a side note, Joshu was asked about the story I just told you, the robe story of the 6P (the 6th Patriarch).

> **A monk asked, "Having chased him [6P] all the way to Mount T'a-sou, why didn't he pick them up?"**
> **Joshu picked up the hem of his robe and said, "Where can you get this?"**
> **The monk said, "I'm not asking about this one."**
> **Joshu said, "In that case, you can't pick it up."[20]**

This sort of talking is a tradition of Zen Masters. When we read about the Buddhisms in books or listen to Dogen Buddhism masters talk, we can hear that Dogen's followers make a great effort to be understood. There is no such effort by Zen Masters. If any understanding were sufficient to carry you through Gate of Enlightenment then there would be no Zen.

Most people do not read the conversations of the Zen Masters, instead they read the writings of the Buddhisms or academics who write for a living and thus form ideas about what Zen is that are perhaps not entirely accurate. Spend any time with a Zen Master and you will give up entirely on forming ideas.

---

[19] p50 "The Zen Teaching of Huang-Po: On the Transmission of Mind: John ..." <http://www.amazon.com/Zen-Teaching-Huang-Po-Transmission-Mind/dp/0802150926>

[20] #185, "The Recorded Sayings of Zen Master Joshu: James Green, Kreido ..." <http://www.amazon.com/Recorded-Sayings-Zen-Master-Joshu/dp/157062870X>

Nothing holy in Zen

**A monk asked Ummon, "What is the Buddha?"
Ummon answered, "A shit wiping stick."[21]**

Some might say that Ummon is being contrary or deliberately inflammatory, or that a shit wiping stick is useful, thus Buddha is useful. Others might argue that Buddha's place in Zen is not one of extraordinary esteem, thus Ummon is extraordinarily demoting Buddha to compensate for the Buddha-worship that is so prevalent. None of these answers are Zen. Who is to say that Buddha is not a shit wiping stick? Where does metaphor end and authority begin?

This is the first challenge that all religions face, where to put authority... *Who to believe.* Once they figure that out, then whoever they pick, however it is preserved, these become special and sacred, with a special and sacred meaning. Worshiping the sacred takes a great many forms, from making the sacred the focus of prayer or meditation to revering the sacred in practices and behavior. If you can put it on a bumper sticker, it's sacred. Different kinds of Buddhists have different kinds of sacred and different attitudes toward their own sacred and their rival's sacred.

Zen, on the other hand, has nothing sacred. Not Buddha, not the Patriarchs and the Masters. Not Zen sayings, not the Transmission. Everything is fair game for mockery, negation, and outright lack of interest in Zen. A student of Joshu's was once asked about his teacher's famous Mu koan, and the student replied

---

[21] "Zen and Zen Classics: Vol 4 Mumonkan - R.H. Blyth... - Google Books."
<http://books.google.com/books/about/Zen_and_Zen_Classics_Mumonkan.html?id=B3zXAAAAMAAJ>

something like, *You slander my teacher, he had no such koan*. If your students don't consider you sacred, then that's Zen. If your students revere you, then that's one of the Buddhisms, perhaps Dogen Buddhism.

Ryutan's Candle is a particularly interesting Case in Mumonkan. It discusses enlightenment (not through sitting) and study, knowledge (and its error) and especially what is taught in Zen. Mumon's commentary is one long complaint about the people in the Case, their words and conduct, what they would have better said or done, and closes with:

"Looking at the whole affair impartially, it was all just a farce."

This is what it all comes to in Zen, mockery and criticism of everything, even the very koans that you chose yourself to teach your students by means of. Ha! A revolution against even the revolution. Do not stop! Do not hesitate! Revolt!

Mockery is one of the great Zen traditions. Huang Po did it, Joshu did it, and Mumon did it. Once you laugh at something it is hard to revere it, once you make fun of something it is difficult to maintain the illusion of its holiness. If the Pope traveled around doing stand-up comedy, even stand-up about Catholicism, the Catholic Church would be diminished in the eyes of many people.

So, Ummon has no reverence for Buddha, the Masters have no reverence for the Patriarchs, the students have no reverence for the teachers. This is the Zen way. Can the same be said of any of the Buddhist religions? The followers of Dogen Buddhism are particularly respectful, authority is in the clothing and manner, in the structure of the ranks. How can Zen be in any way related to the religions with their sacred this and that? Ridiculous.

No dogmas, no Transmission

When we ask the question "What do Christians believe?" there are a flood of answers. When we ask the question, "What do Buddhists believe?" there are even more answers, few of them the same, but there are still *answers*. When we go to the lineage of Zen Masters and ask this question, we get nothing much.

Whatever answer people give to this question "What do you believe" is the dogma of that person. When enough people share a dogma, then this is the basis of a religion and that religion is defined by the collective dogma of its followers, or, in most cases today, by the religious hierarchy of officials who enforce and maintain the dogma. Since Buddhism is undefined and fractured, that is "poorly officiated", there is a wide variety of dogma. The Dogen Buddhism religion has its dogma, much of it centered on Zazen meditation, how to do it, the belief that doing it is the enlightenment, and the belief that the benefits accrued through meditation are not the enlightenment of the religion. All this is dogma.

Zen has no dogma. Even the dogma "no dogma" is not the dogma of Zen, just as Huang Po said earlier. But he goes farther than that even! Huang Po also says something about the Zen Transmission which is interesting, and sets it apart from other transmissions, like the Soto/Dogen Buddhism transmission.

"Obtaining no Dharma whatever is called Mind transmission. The understanding of this Mind implies no Mind and no Dharma." - Huang Po

One reason to start with Huang Po is that he is so old. He lived and taught three generations after the Sixth Patriarch, so his teaching is one of the anchor points (historically) for the beginning of Zen. Those that followed, Joshu for example, echoed Huang Po's stance on questions of dogma and transmission in their own way. Or perhaps they were all echoing the 6P. Or perhaps they were all echoing Bodhidharma.

Another academic question about Zen dogma or lack thereof is that certainly up to 6P there is evidence of tampering with the texts that have been handed down. Scholars argue that the authenticity of the Platform Sutra is an open question, and D.T. Suzuki claims that within a single generation after 6P the Platform Sutra had already been rewritten. So, old is not necessarily true, and besides, this is Zen. What does it matter what anyone says? Unless they say, "This matters" in which case it isn't Zen, is it? So Zen has no dogma and cannot be counted as a part of the group of religions of Buddhism which all have dogma. Likewise, those who follow Dogen Buddhism have a dogma about their practice, and anything with a dogma is not Zen.

Religion and Philosophy are not Zen

Alan Watts says this in his famous book *The Way of Zen,* "Zen is a way and a view of life which does not belong to any of the formal categories of modern Western thought. It is not a religion or a philosophy; it is not a psychology or a type of science."[22]

As to his credentials, Watts says that he is not "a Zennist or even a Buddhist." More to the point though, Watts talks about his experience as a sort of Zen researcher.

---

[22] "The Way of Zen: Alan W. Watts: 9780375705106: Amazon.com: Books." 2006. 24 Jan. 2013 <http://www.amazon.com/Way-Zen-Alan-W-Watts/dp/0375705104>

"I have based the essential view of Zen here presented upon a careful study of the more important of its early Chinese records" and also "my information is derived from a large number of personal encounters with teachers and students of Zen, spread over more than twenty years."

This is interesting because Watts is a Westerner, an outsider to both Chinese and Japanese culture, who formed his views on Zen based on travel and study. His observations of what is not Zen are based on his examination of the subject more for himself, more impartially than, say, Buddhists. In any case Watts is well respected, so I include him as an appeal to authority.

A monk asked, "How should one act during every hour of the day such that the ancestors are not betrayed?"

Ummon said, "Give up your effort."

The monk said, "How should I give up my effort?"

Ummon said, "Give up the words you just uttered."

· Actions do not impart Zen
· The pursuit of such ideas is not Zen (ie. the idea that ancestors would be betrayed by a deviation applies a false absolute)

3. Mindfulness is not Zen

Southeast Asia is well represented in the Buddhist and Dogen Buddhism community. Thich Nhat Hanh is one of the more famous examples. Thich talks a good deal about mindfulness, not so much about Zen history or the Zen Masters. I recently googled Thich Nhat Hanh and Bodhidharma, but didn't find very much. Then I googled Thich Nhat Hahn and Buddha... jackpot. For an informal survey it was surprisingly indicative of the focus of Thich's thinking, of the focus of the tradition that he is a part of, Buddhism's Dogen Buddhism.

Whenever I encounter Thich in speeches or books, or any of the Southeast Asia Dogen Buddhisms, I don't find any of the Zen memes. Certainly Zen could be transmitted without the lineage or the memes, I don't mean to suggest that, but the memes grew out of what these old men *pointed to*. Dogen's followers and the Southeast Asian Buddhisms don't point, they instruct. Just read what they say... it isn't even vaguely related. Some of it sounds like Zen, but then misses by a single hair. This missing by a single hair is called "not even vaguely related."

For example, Huang Po is repeating the Sixth Patriarch when he says,

> "To hold that there is something born and try to eliminate it, that is to fall among [those who seek to overcome their ordinary living in order to enter Nirvana]."[23]

Mindfulness does not directly attach itself to something born, but certainly this forcing the mind away from somewhere and into the

---

[23] p44 "The Zen Teaching of Huang-Po: On the Transmission of Mind: John ..." <http://www.amazon.com/Zen-Teaching-Huang-Po-Transmission-Mind/dp/0802150926>

now of doing dishes or whatever, this is eliminating something, namely the wandering that the mind was doing before it became mindful.

Mindfulness is closely related to peacefulness which is not Zen either. Why would anyone desire peace? That people desire peace is just as much a problem as people desiring money or power or a fight. Huang Po says this about it:

> **There is no 'wrong desire', no 'anger', no 'hatred', no 'love', no 'victory', no 'failure'.**[24]

Anyone who reads Huang Po should have an interesting conversation with Thich about it sometime. If Bodhidharma were to have that conversation I would guess there would be a bunch of "No" in there. As a footnote, all the habitual meditators I've encountered have been remarkably gentle and peaceful people on the whole. Of course take that away from them and you'll see a different side of things.

Being "in the moment" is not Zen

The present is not more important than the past or less important, reverie is not good or bad, paying attention to where you are is no more important than paying attention to what you remember. Zen Masters have given a few examples of the Zen perspective on being in the moment, apart from a general chorus of condemnation for "pious practices" by which I take them to mean "anything you do in a church" as opposed to chopping wood and carrying water which you do ordinarily.

---

[24] p88 "The Zen Teaching of Huang-Po: On the Transmission of Mind: John ..." <http://www.amazon.com/Zen-Teaching-Huang-Po-Transmission-Mind/dp/0802150926>

"The entirety of the past and present are in me."[25]

Joshu is answering a question about who can transmit the Dharma now that Buddha is dead. He doesn't seem too concerned about it, moreover he is generally not concerned with getting rid of the past at all. Mumon says that if you pass the Gate you can hear with the ears of the Zen Masters and Patriarchs, and see with their eyes. This in the moment nonsense separates out this moment from the last one, attaches to this moment in a perpetual delight of self-conscious perception.

We could say that "chop wood, carry water" is being in the moment, but of course then it would be "chop wood, carry water, in the moment." Not quite the same thing. Of course the distinction is either nonsense or nonsensical to people who don't see the "*trying* to be" in the "*being in*." Even if you think you aren't trying because you are busy *being in*, you still started off in the wrong direction and thus are unlikely to not get anywhere.

People have talked about being in the zone, enjoying the moment, living in the present or the now as what they think of as Zen. Certainly Zen Masters manifest this in the spontaneity that they display. Once again though this mistakes the effect for the cause. Someone who is free is likely to be very here and now. Someone who is trying to be very here and now is likely not free. They are bound by their trying, bound by the desire to be here and now. Bound by their own idea of what Zen should be.

---

[25] #159, "The Recorded Sayings of Zen Master Joshu: James Green, Kreido ..." <http://www.amazon.com/Recorded-Sayings-Zen-Master-Joshu/dp/157062870X>

34

If 'there's never been a single thing', past, present and future are meaningless.[26] - Huang Po

Where and when have nothing to do with Zen. By teaching people to be here now, Thich encourages them to discipline their minds in the same way that meditation disciplines the mind. Read Huang Po! Where is this discipline in his teaching? In any of the teachings of the Zen Masters? This idea that the mind is a dog to be trained and commanded is from the Buddhisms, specifically, but from all the religions in general. It is nonsense of course, just another desire born of the endless engine of desire, just another attachment. Thich is not a Zen Master at all, but a Buddhist. This is why you can read a whole book of his and never hear a single Zen Master's name. Thich is creating, as all the religions do, in order to keep their dogma fresh and accessible. He is a kind and pleasant man. Who were the kind and pleasant Zen Masters?

Here is another old man, what does he say about this past and present and future nonsense? His name is P'ang Yun:

The past is already past-
Don't try to regain it.
The present does not stay-
Don't try to touch it from moment to moment.
The future is not come-

---

[26]p110 "The Zen Teaching of Huang-Po: On the Transmission of Mind: John ..." <http://www.amazon.com/Zen-Teaching-Huang-Po-Transmission-Mind/dp/0802150926>

Don't think about it beforehand...
Whatsoever comes to eye leave it be.
There are no commandments to be kept,
There is no filth to be cleansed.[27]

"The present doesn't stay" but, on the other hand, you can keep trying to grasp at it forever! Religions depend on this sort of thing, grasping at the unattainable rather than what people normally grasp at, money, power, fame. The futility of chasing the unattainable is a great convincer of the "truth" that the religions are selling. Of course they create this futility themselves, with their values and virtues and dogmas and doctrines and whatnot. No freedom there, but plenty of grasping, plenty of futility.

Gradual Attainment is not Zen

The gospel on meditation is that the enlightenment is the practice. This is not Zen. The Zen Masters, certainly from Hui-neng on, were very definite that Zen enlightenment is not an activity, but a suddenness, happening in the blink of an eye. One of the early quotes is Huang Po's knife thrust, here is Huang Po on the blink of an eye:

"Though others may talk of the Way of the Buddhas as something to be reached by various pious practices and by sutra-study, you must have nothing to do with such ideas. A perception, sudden as blinking, that subject

---

[27] p21 "Crazy Clouds: Zen Radicals, Rebels & Reformers: Perle Besserman ..." <http://www.amazon.com/Crazy-Clouds-Radicals-Rebels-Reformers/dp/0877735433>

and object are one, will lead to a deeply mysterious wordless understanding."[28]

Dogen Buddhism religions rely on the benefits of meditation, proven medical benefits like any exercise, while cutting off the mind to produce a sort of waking state of detachment. This state of detachment requires Zazen meditation to be maintained, but to many this detachment looks like what some imagine that Zen Masters look like.

Some will say that it isn't true detachment; that the Zazen meditation lifestyle is one in which there is an acceptance of suffering. But this acceptance requires regular doses of Zazen meditation in order to be maintained. So, the acceptance is based on dependence, how is that freedom?

How can there be any other freedom? That is why Zen is so interesting in the first place. How can freedom without detachment be possible? This is what Bodhidharma preached though, freedom; Not detachment, not Zazen meditation, not tolerance.

---

[28] p92 "The Zen Teaching of Huang-Po: On the Transmission of Mind: John ..." <http://www.amazon.com/Zen-Teaching-Huang-Po-Transmission-Mind/dp/0802150926>

Interlude:

Ummon held up his staff, and said, "We are told in the scriptures that an ordinary man thinks the staff is a real existence; that those of Hinayana take it as nothing; that those believing in the pratyekabuddha take it as an illusory existence; that bodhisattvas say its reality is emptiness. But I say to you, take the staff as just a staff[29];

· By defining it as itself no real truth is established
· The lack of defining truth is a Zen hallmark.

---

[29] Zen and Zen Classics, Vol.2, R.H. Blyth; p.132

4. Sitting Meditation is not Dhyana, Ch'an, or Zen

In a lecture I mentioned earlier John Peacock says, "meditation" is a very interesting word... there is no such word as meditation in the lexicon of early Buddhism... Buddhists do not meditate... they cultivate, as in do something with the intention of bringing something into the world."[30] The word "meditation" is one of the translation errors that Peacock argues has been perpetuated since the 1800s when the West began to look East.

So when we read about the sorts of mental cultivation that Zen Masters practice we have to acknowledge that there are many sorts of mental cultivation, some involve sitting, others do not. Many Zen Masters practiced some form of mental cultivation, some refer to the cultivation of the ordinary, day-to-day mind that chops wood and carries water. Some Zen Masters certainly did sitting cultivations, who knows what they were thinking? None of the Zen Masters taught sitting contemplation as part of any path to enlightenment. There are no koans from Zen Masters which involve sitting meditation or Zazen meditation as an element of enlightenment, there are no lectures by Zen Masters encouraging enlightenment.

Part of the meditation reputation of Zen, apart from the aggressive proselytizing of the Dogen Buddhism crowd, comes from a nickname that Bodhidharma was given, "wall-gazer". According to the myth, Bodhidharma stared at the wall for nine years after he arrived in China. D.T. Suzuki, who read more than most of us, relates this from the Pieh Chi:

---

[30] m18:00 Uncertain Minds: How the West Misunderstands Buddhism
[30] <https://www.youtube.com/watch?v=hXYBtT4uN30&feature>

"The master first stayed in the Shorinji monastery for nine years, and when he taught the second patriarch, it was only in the following way: 'Externally keep yourself away from all relationships, and, internally, have no hankerings in your heart; *when your mind is like unto a straight standing wall you may enter into the Path.* Hui-k'e tried variously to explain the reason of mind, but failed to realize the truth itself. The master simply said, 'No! No!' and never proposed to explain to his disciple what was the mind-essence in its thought-less state. [Later] said Hui-k'e, 'I know now how to keep myself away from all relationships.' 'You make it a total annihilation, do you not?' queried the master. 'No master,' replied Hui-k'e, 'I do not make it a total annihilation.' 'How do you testify to your statement?' 'For I know it always in a most intelligible manner, but to express it in words- that is impossible." 'That is the mind-essence itself transmitted by all the Buddhas. Harbour no doubts about it.'

① Totality would be an absolute (e the epiphny is not verbally conveyable

This passage is interesting in several ways. Not only does it give a different account of the "wall gazing" nickname and the fury that Bodhidharma's teaching excited in the Buddhist community, it also represents the core of D.T. Suzuki's perspective on Zen as the real Buddhism. Also, interestingly, again we find the meme of Negation, "No! No!" as the only teaching.

The Zen anti-meditative-enlightenment perspective is next apparent in the writings of the Sixth Patriarch, who, again according to the story, received the title over a senior monk Shen Hsiu. Shen Hsiu is said to be of "the Northern School" that favored meditation, as opposed to the Sixth Patriarch's "Southern

School." There is a good deal of argument about this, in part because the Sixth Patriarch's Platform Sutra is so long and so varied in style and content. Here, though, is Huang Po's take on it, who was three generations removed from the Sixth Patriarch, and whose writings were much less of a political battleground after his death:

> **Monk: Why did [Elder Shen Hsiu] not receive the robe [from the Fifth Patriarch]?**
>
> **Huang Po: Because he still indulged in conceptual thought- in a dharma of activity. To him, 'as you practice, so shall you attain' was a reality.[31]**

Actions and objects are without meaning

Dharma of activity. Some people have a peculiar sort of faith that claims that doing something (Zazen meditation) can be transformed, via mental powers, into a non-doing "just being". This is a tenet of the Zazen meditation faith, that this special kind of doing is not actual doing. This tenet is required in order to appear to conform with the general Zen teaching against intentional pursuit of enlightenment. Without this faith of course, anybody walking by would say to themselves, ah! someone meditating. Even if, as it turns out, the somebody walking by was a Zen Master. In Zen, doing is doing. Pretending to not be doing while doing is still just doing.

Huang Po is an aggressive inheritor of the Sixth Patriarch's admonitions against meditation. Here are a few examples which are echoed down through the lineage:

---

[31] p64 "The Zen Teaching of Huang-Po: On the Transmission of Mind: John ..." <http://www.amazon.com/Zen-Teaching-Huang-Po-Transmission-Mind/dp/0802150926>

"By thinking of something you create an entity and by thinking of nothing you create another."[32]

Here Huang Po is steering students away from whatever the mind can *do*, because *doing* is not Zen. Huang Po is really on echoing the Sixth Patriarch's "nothing from the first" teaching on the subject which 6P used to counter this idea in meditation that the mirror of the mind is polished to remove imperfection. 6P said there is no mirror, no dirt, no reason to polish.

"A conscious lack of... intention, or even a consciousness that you do *not* have *no* such intention, will be sufficient to deliver you into the demon's power. But they will not be demons from the outside; they will be the self-creations of your own mind."[33]

Huang Po is brought back to this question again and again, as other Zen Masters were, because of the prevalence and seductiveness of meditation as a means to enlightenment. Zen Masters were after *freedom of mind*, a freedom even beyond the desire for meditation as an escape from suffering

"Bodhidharma pointed directly to the truth that all sentient beings have always been of one substance with the Buddha. He did not follow any of those mistaken 'methods of attainment'."

---

[32] p86 "The Zen Teaching of Huang-Po: On the Transmission of Mind: John ..." <http://www.amazon.com/Zen-Teaching-Huang-Po-Transmission-Mind/dp/0802150926>

[33] p104 "The Zen Teaching of Huang-Po: On the Transmission of Mind: John ..." <http://www.amazon.com/Zen-Teaching-Huang-Po-Transmission-Mind/dp/0802150926>

As a closing comment, Huang Po like other Zen Masters, emphasizes Bodhidharma as the beginning of the Zen lineage. This is likely in part because of Bodhidharma's "no method of attainment" emphasis began with him. Possibly from Huang Po's perspective there was great debate in the Chinese world about what Buddha's legacy was and who could claim it, but at the time comparatively less about Bodhidharma's legacy.

Zazen Sitting Meditation: Authoritarian Quietism

A well regarded book in some circles that bears on this subject is from a much different Suzuki named Shunryu Suzuki. Shunryu wrote a book called, "Zen Mind, Beginner's Mind" in which he expounds the importance of meditation and talks about how Zazen meditation is the core of Zen. This is Dogen Buddhism, and this is doubly clear when we look at what else Shunryu has to say.

First, Shunryu mixes in some traditional Zen phrases and this might be confusing at first until you realize he is just repeating them without putting himself in their context. When he isn't mildly peppering his teachings with Zen that he ignores, he will repeat something and then ignore it shortly thereafter without noticing it. Citing the cart and horse metaphor from a koan about meditation not being Zen, he goes on to say later that the cart and horse are no different... as if the Zen Master he is quoting couldn't tell the difference.

The context Shunryu chooses for himself is *purity*. There is no purity in Zen, there is nothing to be pure, but for Shunryu purity is essential. Shunryu wants us to pursue mental purity which is clouded by our thinking, so we must "calm" and pacify

43

our minds to experience this purity. He says, "When your practice becomes effortless, you can stop your mind."[34] This is not Zen.

Second, Shunryu is very clear that Buddha is the foundation of his teaching, and this teaching is based on **having someone teach you the sitting posture**. "Actually, we are not the Soto school at all. We are just Buddhists. We are not even Zen Buddhists."[35] He goes on, same page, to say

> "...according to Dogen, his way was not one of the many schools [of Buddhism]. If this is so, you may ask why we put emphasis on the sitting posture or why we put emphasis on having a teacher. The reason is because Zazen is not just one of the four ways of behavior... sitting cannot be compared to the other four activities."

Zazen meditation, Dogen, this is having a teacher teach you to sit. That is the core of what this religion, this branch of Buddhism, is about. When you accept the faith, then of course the doctrine will be expanded, just as with any religion. We are fortunate that Shunryu was willing to cut through all that.

"Special Knowledge" is not Zen

Special knowledge is a fundamental element of all of the religions, religions that pose as the authority necessary to understand their holy text. Since none of us were there when these koans were uttered all of it is hearsay. When someone tells you they have secret knowledge that explains the true intent or the true meaning or the real point of a case or koan, then nod politely and

---

[34] p41 "Zen Mind, Beginner's Mind: Shunryu Suzuki, David Chadwick ..."

[35] p125"Zen Mind, Beginner's Mind: Shunryu Suzuki, David Chadwick..."

say "not Zen." If you want you can add, "Likely one of the Buddhisms."

There is no need for anyone to explain the "true meaning" of Joshu's Mu to you. Ah ha! you say, but you explain it (Well, chapter 6). I am just teasing you. Joshu's NO is not an explanation, this is just a translation problem. So Ha! You have been taken in (by yourself). In any case the rest of the koans are just the same. No one can explain Ryutan's candle to you, and if anyone does then that is not Zen. Arguing over the word for "candle" hardly qualifies as an explanation.

Zen Masters, including Mumon, never explained anything. Read Mumonkan, written for novice students and full of "teachings" on the koans. If you learn a single thing then you should write a book yourself.

All meditation is just exercise and thus Not Zen

If someone began preaching a religion that involved jogging, but told people is was za-jogging and said that za-jogging is not in any way jogging, because in jogging you run somewhere and in za-jogging you run nowhere, so it isn't really jogging, would you believe them? Zazen meditation is in the same boat. It is sitting meditation that people believe, for reasons of faith, isn't really sitting meditation. People believe it's different because, though they are physically doing meditation, they are taking it on faith that when they really just do it they aren't meditating. It's a faith thing, like all the religions have. Something you have to agree to in order for the worship to make sense. Only Zazen meditation practitioners call the worship practice. Zazen meditation has really taken off in the West, a culture with a large population of conflicted worshipers.

45

There are many studies on meditation that indicate that meditation has a measurable effect on the neurological system. My bet is, and I'll put the profits of this book up against this, is that no matter what kind of meditation people practice, no matter if they call it Zazen meditation or Transcendental Meditation or Buddhist meditation, when we hook these people up to brain scanners and run some blood work it will all look the same. Meditation is good for you if you use it with care, like jogging. Meditation is not Zen.

Zen Masters who said Meditation is Not Zen

There are many examples of Zen Masters warning against meditation and the detachment tolerance that it produces. Zazen meditation advocates will argue that Zazen meditation isn't meditation, but their argument relies on their religious faith, not on any objective premise, much like one religion arguing that their prayer is not the same as other faiths. This is one of the most famous koans, explicitly separating enlightenment and meditation. Eno, the Sixth Patriarch, also known as Hui-neng, is so central to Zen that there is no one to my knowledge that claims to be a Zen teacher that doesn't claim Eno as part of their lineage. What does Hui-neng say about meditation?

> **Jinshu [Northern School] used to tell his disciples to concentrate their minds on quietness, to sit doing meditation for a long time, and not to lie down as far as possible. One of these disciples went to Eno [the Sixth Patriarch] and asked him about it. Eno said, "To concentrate the mind on quietness is a disease of the mind, and not Zen at all. What an idea, restricting the**

body to sitting all the time! That is useless. Listen to my verse:

> **To sit and not lie down during one's life-time**
> **To lie and never sit during one's death-time,**
> **Why should we thus task**
> **This stinking bag of bones?"**

"To concentrate the mind on quietness is a disease of the mind." How much clearer does it need to be? Zen Masters said this was "Quietism" and said that it was "false Zen", a "disease" and not Zen. How does the Dogen Buddhism crowd get around this? They say they aren't concentrating on anything, they are just watching... quietly. Hence the description "Quietism" still applies, doesn't it?

Baso is another famous Zen Master. His teacher Nanyue acts out the problem with Zazen meditation/quietism in pantomime! It still isn't enough:

> **Zen master (Baso) was an attendant to Nanyue and personally received the mind seal from him, exceeding his peers. Before that, he lived in Kaiyuan Monastery and did Zazen all day long. Knowing that Baso was a dharma vessel, Nanyue went to him and asked, "Great monastic, what do you intend by doing Zazen?" Baso said, "I am intending to be a buddha." Nanyue picked up a brick and started polishing it. Baso said, "What are you doing?" Nanyue said," I am trying to make a mirror," Baso said, "How can you make a mirror by polishing a brick?" Nanyue said, "How can you become a buddha by doing Zazen?" Baso said, "What do you mean by that?" Nanyue said, "Think about driving a**

47

cart. **When it stops moving, do you whip the cart or the horse?" Baso said nothing. Nanyue said, "Do you want to practice sitting Zen or sitting Buddha? If you understand sitting Zen, you will know that Zen is not about sitting or lying down. If you want to learn sitting Buddha, know that sitting Buddha is without any fixed form. Do not use discrimination in the non- abiding dharma. If you practice sitting as Buddha, you must kill Buddha.' If you are attached to the sitting form, you are not yet mastering the essential principle." Baso heard this admonition and felt as if he had tasted sweet nectar.**

The sitting form is not an appropriate definition of either parent.

One of the marvelous pieces of mental gymnastics that Shunryu produces in his book "Zen Mind, Beginner's Mind" is when, in trying to reconcile his Zazen meditation with Baso's lesson about the brick, he says, "the cart and the horse are just the same." The reason I like this so much is that Zen Masters use this structure all the time in the Negation meme; Enlightenment is the same as unenlightened, the Master is the same as the student or the fool, the ordinary mind is the same as the enlightened mind. Zen Masters are negating the imagination that conceives of something beyond with this technique, negating the Dream of Change. In what possible analogy can the cart and the horse be the same and there still be any analogy at all? Shunryu is a pleasant enough man, pleasant in the way that all meditation addicts are pleasant, but his mind is trapped just the same.

I would also point out that all the koans of the Zen Masters that talk about enlightenment feature enlightenment in odd circumstances, but I have yet to come across one that features an enlightenment that is the oneness-with-practice from Zazen meditation. Why do you suppose that is, if Zazen meditation or meditation is so central to Zen? I am sure there is an intriguing answer to that somewhere in the Dogen Buddhism community, but I haven't come across it yet.

Just as Huang Po said earlier, non-action is a form of creation the same as action. You can't negate your way out of that! Why? Negation is a tool that eliminates illusion. When you try to use this tool on reality, the reality that *what you do* is still you *doing something* regardless of what sacred name you give it, negation fails you. There are many cases or koans where students claim to not be or have or do, yet are suddenly revealed by the Master as having faked it through pretend negation.

Here is a famous example:

> **When the Tesshu, a master of Zen, calligraphy and swordsmanship, was a young man he called on the Zen master Dokuon. Wishing to impress Dokuon he said, "The mind, the Buddha, and all sentient beings after all do not exist. The true nature of phenomenon is emptiness. There is no realization, no delusion, no sagacity, no mediocrity, nothing to give and nothing to receive.**
> **Dokuon promptly hit him with a bamboo stick. Tesshu became quite furious.**
> **Dokuon said quietly: "If nothing exists, where did this anger come from?"[36]** LOL

---

[36]http://www.abuddhistlibrary.com/Buddhism/C%20-%20Zen/Stories/Eleven%20Zen%20Stories/Zen%20Stories%20-%20Seishinkan%20Bujitsu.htm

What is there is there, there is no negating it. Ummon made this same point, not always by hitting people.

So, the student claims to have seen into all this nothing, and yet when struck with the pipe the foolishness of his negation materializes. Ha! This same technique works with the Zazen meditation crowd. As soon as they are challenged to give up Zazen meditation, all the supposed negation of their attachment to it vanishes. When asked what would happen if they gave it up for a month the relatively honest ones will admit to unhappiness at the prospect. The others, well, they won't even consider giving it up!

Mumon makes it even simpler, but this only got his book banned and some of his readers excommunicated from the Soto school of Dogen Buddhism. In the end they recanted, but in some ways the damage was done. Here are three relevant warnings.

Mumon's Warnings;
    1. To follow the compass and keep to the rule is to tie oneself without rope.
    3. To unify and pacify the mind is quietism, and false Zen.[37]
    9. Sitting blankly in Zen practice is the condition of a dean man.[38]

    dud

What is the rule? Any rule. Like "Zazen is Zen." What is the compass? Anything that tells you where to go. Like a teacher or a priest. You might ask, how is anyone to learn anything about Zen if there is no following rules and listening to teachers? Remember

---

[37] Mumonkan, any version. Free online several places.

[38] Mumonkan, Appendix, Mumon's Zen Warnings.

the title of the book? The pursuit of Zen is a revolution against everything. Every rule. Every teacher. Even against revolution itself. If you think you learned something about Zen from this book, then throw it into the fire.

Behind every religion there is a reason for you to need that religion, a reason to believe whatever it is that they tell you. In the case of the Buddhisms, there is a bit of original sin. The idea is that the confusion of the mind clouds the purity of the "true self" and if you polish the mirror of the mind to remove the impurity then you will find your true self. Hui-neng, the Sixth Patriarch of Zen, was discarding this notion with his catch phrase, "Nothing from the first." Other Zen Masters teach this also, because, really, you have to believe in something to argue that there is something to believe in.

Huang Po: Since you are fundamentally complete in every respect, you should not try to supplement that perfection by such meaningless practices.

IE. Anyone capable of thought can achieve an epiphany

For Huang Po, "meaningless practices" are more or less anything you do in the name of enlightenment, chanting, praying, meditating, memorizing sacred texts, and so on. There is an idea in some of the Buddhisms that this sort of thing is helpful, or even meritorious. There is nothing meritorious or helpful in Zen, not even talking to Zen Masters. Huang Po has some suggestions, they all do, although all of them involve seeing, rather than doing or not doing.

It bears repeating that several different Chinese words are translated uniformly as "meditation" in a great many texts. When the Zen Masters warn against Quietism it can be difficult to figure out what exactly they are talking about. This is doubly difficult in that there is a strong advocacy group proclaiming that Zazen [meditation] is Zen and Zen is Zazen [meditation]. From my perspective this is enough to reject Zazen meditation, for the rest of you there is both the original text and the context of the word in translated text.

Suzuki's book on the Platform Sutra, *The Zen Doctrine of No-Mind*, offers a very detailed interpretation of the word choices that provides insight into the Sixth Patriarch's views on Quietism. One particular passage captures several aspects of the problem.

K'an-ching means 'to keep an eye on purity'... a quietistic contemplation of one's self-nature or self-being. D.T. Suzuki

"K'an-ching" is one of the Chinese words sometimes translated as meditation. Here Suzuki is saying that this particular word is actually a Chinese phrase used to describe an action with a specific purpose. Regardless of how we interpret the action, as a doing or a not-doing or however, this idea that quietly contemplating the self-nature is not Zen.

Suzuki goes on to describe the situation in Hui-neng's time and before, the popularity of Zazen meditation and other quiet meditations in the Buddhist community. Today many people think that Zen is just another flavor of Buddhism, but Bodhidharma and Hui-neng were not so popular among Buddhists in their day. Buddhists were skeptical that Zen was even a kind of Buddhism. Part of this is the direct result of Bodhidharma and his lineage rejecting the inner essence of Buddhist meditation, the very sort of meditation that Buddhists and the Dogen Buddhisms practice today and teach as the fundamental essence of their religions.

Honorable Mention, Alan Watts

I am surprised by the continuing popularity and the almost teen idol following of Alan Watts among many people who are interested in the Zen path. While Watts may have assumed a more masterful image in the minds of his readers than he intended, he nevertheless is an honest examiner of the Zen debate. In his book *The Way of Zen* he talks honestly about his errors and mistakes in his earlier book. How many authors are so honest about any topic, let alone one which is clearly so personal to both author and reader?

For this reason, and as an appeal to authority, I offer you Alan Watts' view of meditation from *The Way of Zen*, which he based on his own interviews, reading, and research:

> Alan Watts: "Nowhere in doctrine of all the T'ang masters have I been able to find any instructions in or recommendation of the type of za-Zen which is today the principal occupation of Zen monks. On the contrary, the practice is discussed time after time in the apparently negative fashion."

Those who follow Dogen and those that have converted to the Southeast Asian religions of course have little interest in Watts. There is a segment of the community in the West that has a great respect from Mr. Watts, and his view that Zazen meditation is not a Zen Master invention might inform their view of what has become the defining practice of the several Buddhism churches.

One day Ummon ascended the rostrum and said, "Vasubandhu happened to transform himself into a staff of chestnut wood, and, striking the earth once, all the innumerable Buddhas were released from their entangling words." So saying he descended from the pulpit.

5. Bonus Chapter

Here are some random odds and ends that have been brought up here or somewhere else. Don't be picky. There is no pickiness in Zen.

The Rinzai Sect of Zen

First let me introduce you to Rinzai. He was one of the old men, nothing unusual about him, nothing special. Joshu went to see Rinzai, but Joshu went to see everyone, traveling around and challenging their Zen until Joshu was eighty.

> **Rinzai came after Joshu, considered lineally, but Joshu nevertheless went to see him. Rinzai was washing his feet. Joshu asked him, "What is the meaning of Daruma's coming from the West?" that is, what is the essence of Buddhism?**
>
> **This is the question solved by Rinzai when beaten by his master Obaku, and Joshu probably asked it ironically. Glaring at Joshu, Rinzai answered him, "At the moment I am washing my feet!" Joshu leaned forward with the appearance of not hearing what Rinzai had said. Rinzai exclaimed, "Do you want a second ladle of dirty water poured over you?" and Joshu went off.[39]**

In the Sayings of Joshu, this exchange has Rinzai visiting Joshu. What does that say? As far as the record goes, the Rinzai

---

[39] "Zen & Zen Classics by R.H. Blyth..." 2009. 1 Feb. 2013
<http://www.goodreads.com/book/show/1617416.Zen_Zen_Classics>

sect of Zen is the last of the surviving lineages but this doesn't amount to much. I know nothing of Rinzai Zen, East or West, but nevertheless I have heard whispers of Rinzai School not Zen from a few sources I've encountered. Blyth said Rinzai's sect had a bench of Zen that wasn't wide, but it was deep. He made this comment in one of his books so I guess his view was formed in the 1940's or 50's. I've encountered voices who claimed it as a lineage that were... not on any path of Zen. For example, answers to koans. Some have suggested that within Rinzai a student can be "passed" on koans by a Master, and allowed to "progress on" in the study of other koans. This is ridiculous. The Zen Masters have been very clear that there is no progress in Zen. Huang Po was very clear about this, at least with regard to the Zen of his lineage:

"This state of being admits of no degrees."[40]

Perhaps there are pockets of Rinzai that have some Zen, perhaps there are those which have transformed into a religion, with knowledge and wisdom accordingly. You can likely find out for yourself.

Alan Watts also makes a curious comment about Rinzai, that students he encountered were "sworn to silence" about their studies. Secrecy is not Zen. What is there to be kept secret? This is as ridiculous as Zazen meditation and those who have put their trust in Watts can hardly do worse than not putting their trust in those who suggest that secrecy has a role in Zen studies.

---

[40] p34"The Zen Teaching of Huang-Po: On the Transmission of Mind: John ..." <http://www.amazon.com/Zen-Teaching-Huang-Po-Transmission-Mind/dp/0802150926>

Nihilism is Not Zen

I add this section because many people, finding themselves accidentally engaged in this conversation, often end up at this point arguing that this reading of the old men that I am putting forward (easier to blame me, rather than them... less reading) inevitably leads to Nihilism. If Zen is not all these friendly things, then it must be the remaining unfriendly thing, Nihilism.

As Zen Masters said many times, good or bad or nihilism are all not Zen. This sort of spectrum of religious beliefs has nothing to do with Zen. It is like asking whether the number zero is tall or short, and when the answer is "no", then arguing that zero must be average height. Zero does not partake of size, and Zen does not partake of good or bad or neither, nihilism. To say there is *something* good or something bad or that *nothing* exists is, in each case, to begin by adding or taking away.

When the monk caught the Sixth Patriarch on the mountain and demanded the robe and bowl of office (This always makes me laugh, what sort of ridiculous office has an official robe and bowl?) and when the monk found he could not take them, he asked for teaching. The Sixth Patriarch told him,

"While you are not thinking of good and not thinking of evil, just at this very moment, return to what you were before your father and mother were born."[41]

This quote is everywhere, a part of the Bodhidharma story, a part of the Zen story. When the Sixth says "Do not think" he is reminding us that good and evil are a thought creation, not an

---

[41] P65"The Zen Teaching of Huang-Po: On the Transmission of Mind: John ..." <http://www.amazon.com/Zen-Teaching-Huang-Po-Transmission-Mind/dp/0802150926>

absolute value. Of course anyone who has ever tried to prove that anything is good or evil knows this.

It is this second line that takes us beyond nihilism, this person (or face) you were before you were born. If you believe in your heart that the only answer is "nothing" then this is where you cast yourself into nihilism. If you believe in your heart that the only answer to this is some sort of person, some spiritual face, then you cast yourself in religions. Why does the Sixth Patriarch ask such a question, if Zen is just nihilism? Or religion?

People often struggle with this question because if what they want to believe is seen to be illusion and what the various authorities of the religions tell them is seen to be illusion, then there is nothing left, and this nothing is called nihilism. But imagination and failing to imagine are both grasping. This Zen the old men talked about *is before conceptual thinking*, before thinking of good and evil, before thinking of nihilism, before thinking of Zazen meditation. I suggest to you that D.T. Suzuki, in his book *The Zen Doctrine of No-mind*, was arguing that this mind of "before thinking" is the meaning of Dhyana that the Sixth Patriarch was pointing to. Read the book yourself, make up your own mind.

Zen is not Taoism

A monk asked, "Without pointing to a Dharma, what is your Dharma?"

Joshu said, "I don't expound the Dharma of the Taoists."

The monk said, "You don't expound the Dharma of the Taoists, but what is your Dharma?"

Joshu said, "I told you, I don't expound the Dharma of the Taoists."

58

The Monk said, "That's it, isn't it?"
Joshu said, "I've never used that to instruct people."[42]

This section is particularly interesting as it follows the section on nihilism. Joshu says that he doesn't expound the Dharma of the Taoists, *as if this negation was a Dharma.* I argued before that the negation of Dharmas was a Dharma and that the negation of the Dharma of Nihilism, if you will, was also a Dharma. As Huang Po said,

"Saying that there is no Dharma to be explained in words is called preaching the Dharma."[43]

Again, Nihilism can be explained in words. Anything that can be explained in words is not the Dharma of Zen. Not Zazen meditation, not mindfulness, not even Taoism which some claim cannot be explained in words. As there are no Taoist Masters, at least in the West, we will have to leave that matter aside until the proper authority can be found.

---

[42] #198 "The Recorded Sayings of Zen Master Joshu: James Green, ..." 2006. <http://www.amazon.com/Recorded-Sayings-Zen-Master-Joshu/dp/157062870X>

[43] p50 "The Zen Teaching of Huang-Po: On the Transmission of Mind ..." <http://www.amazon.com/Zen-Teaching-Huang-Po-Transmission-Mind/dp/0802150926>

Mu-ism: Mu is just No

Many people, or rather many many people, hesitate to translate Joshu's "Mu" from the now famous Case 1 of Mumonkan. Joshu is a simple man, isn't he? Why have so many concluded that he is practicing some mysterious and untranslatable Mu?

This uncertainty is best cleared up by referring to the dialogue in its entirety, which I provide below. Note that Joshu's conversational companion takes the "mu" as "no" with no fuss and bother, and thus he gets two answers for the price of one.

> **A monk asked, "Does a dog have a Buddha nature or not?"**
>
> **The Master said, "Not."**
>
> **The monk said, "Above to all the Buddhas, below to the crawling bugs, all have the Buddha-nature. Why is it that the dog has not?"**
>
> **The master said, "Because he has the nature of karmic delusions."[44]**

Within context it is clear that Joshu's answer is taken, at least by some novice, as a simple "no". Why is there so much fuss about mu then? As far as I can see it is a desire for the mystical and spiritual that drives the mu lovers. Mu reflects the untranslatable, as if there was something about Zen which could be spoken, only not translated. There are no words that describe Zen, translated or untranslated. There is no need for mu just as there is no need for no.

---

[44] #132 "The Recorded Sayings of Zen Master Joshu: James Green, ..." 2006. <http://www.amazon.com/Recorded-Sayings-Zen-Master-Joshu/dp/157062870X>

Here we have Ikan, a student of Baso's, talking about that same dog that Joshu dragged into this. Take heed! Do not lose sight of the Way.

> **Monk: Has the dog the Buddha nature or not?**
> **Ikan: Yes.**
> **Monk: Do you have it or not?**
> **Ikan: I have not.**
> **Monk: All existent creatures have the Buddha-Nature, how is it that you have not?**
> **Ikan: I don't belong to all existent creatures.**
> **Monk: You say you don't belong to all existent creatures. This "You", is it a Buddha or not?**
> **Ikan: It is not a Buddha.**
> **Monk: What sort of thing, in the last resort, is this "You"?**
> **Ikan: It is not a thing.**
> **Monk: Can it be perceived or thought of?**
> **Ikan: Thought cannot attain to it; it cannot be fathomed. For this reason, it is said to be a mystery.[45]**

If you are one of those who understand Joshu's "Mu" then you must easily see through Ikan's "I have not." However, if you find Ikan a stranger then you must realize that Joshu's "Mu" has been mistaken for something other than the Gate of No.

---

[45] p26 "Zen and Zen Classics: Mumonkan - Blyth... - Google Books." 2011.
<http://books.google.com/books/about/Zen_and_Zen_Classics_Mumonkan.html?id=B3zXAAAAMAAJ>

What does the word Zen (or Dhyana) mean?

I mentioned John Peacock earlier (p21), in reference to his discussion of the origin and history of the word "Buddhism". Peacock also argues that "meditation" is a Western word and that it is not found in his survey of early texts regarding Buddha. D.T. Suzuki has a book titled the Zen Doctrine of No-Mind in which Suzuki argues, quite exhaustively, that the Sixth Patriarch of Zen was opposed to meditation and considered Dhyana to mean something other than Western meditation, something translated more like, and I'm paraphrasing, "the mind that answers".

These two aren't the only ones that don't translate Dhyana as the Western word "meditation." In the Sayings of Joshu I came across this dialogue and accompanying footnote, which I've synthesized this way:

> **A monk asked, "What is** the practice of meditation?[46]
> **The master [Joshu] said, "It is not** the practice of meditation.
> **The monk said, "Why is it** 'not the practice of meditation'?"
> **The master said, "It's alive! It's alive!"**[47]

---

[46] The footnote reads as follows: "The Japanese word Zen comes from the Chinese ch'an which comes from the Indian Sanskrit dhyana which means "meditation". The character translated here refers more specifically to the act of doing meditation as a special practice in contrast to the other activities of daily life. Dhyana refers to meditation as a state of mind that is present in all the affairs of daily living."

[47] p42 "The Recorded Sayings of Zen Master Joshu: The First Full English ..." <http://www.amazon.com/The-Recorded-Sayings-Master-Joshu/dp/0761989854>

I suspect that the phrase that Joshu and the monk are using is ts'o chan, which means sitting meditation. The problem that arises is of course that many who teach Zazen meditation believe, as an article of faith, that sitting in Zazen meditation is different than sitting any other kind of meditation. Just like their article of faith that doing Zazen meditation is not "doing", this is silly. But all religions require some sort of mental contortion.

So, three votes against Zen/Ch'an/Dhyana being translated as "meditation." Those who are Alan Watts fans will find his opinion of meditation in *Way of Zen* relevant here. Watts says, "Nowhere in doctrine of all the T'ang masters have I been able to find any instructions in or recommendation of the type of za-Zen which is today the principal occupation of Zen monks. On the contrary, the practice is discussed time after time in the apparently negative fashion". It is unlikely that the T'ang Masters thought of Zen as meaning "meditation" then, and more likely that dhyana is better translated as "that mind present in all the affairs of daily living", not "the mind performing the act of practicing sitting meditation."

Hyakujo's Fox Explained

Hyakujo's fox is the second case in the Mumonkan. It is a very interesting case. Also very funny. I will now reveal all of its secrets. Probably some notable Zen scholars will read this after I am dead and my errors will be the basis of arguments that I never understood anything anyway so let me preface this by saying I never understood anything anyway.

First, there is no old man spirit. Hyakujo was out walking and found a dead fox, and the rest he made up. Second, Zen Masters are not bound by the law of causality or whatever you want to call it. Hyakujo makes this into an error in order to lend credence to his story. Saying they aren't, or saying they are, is just talking anyway.

Third, Hyakujo's student, Huang Po (aka Obaku) sees through the story, hence the question "What if you had answered wrong?" Hyakujo sees through Huang Po, so he invites him to come closer to receive the answer which is going to be a slap. Huang Po sees through Hyakujo's invitation so he slaps Hyakujo first.

Fourth, Hyakujo says something about a Persian and a red beard. This is complicated, but it translates into, "Ha! You, the student, know that I, Hyakujo, am full of monkey poop, which is only possible if you, the student, are full of monkey poop yourself! I salute you as one thrower of monkey poop to another!"

See? All worked out.

Zen Master Suggestions

Some people have asked, "Well, how do we get enlightened if not through Zazen meditation?" Good question, and as Joshu said, "Now, make your bow and depart." I remind you that Joshu also said, "Doing a good thing is not as good as doing nothing." In any case, here's some of the specific guidance I've come across, take it or leave it.

Huang Po:

> **"Were you now to practice keeping your minds motionless at all times, whether walking, standing, sitting or lying; concentrating entirely upon the goal of no thought-creation, no duality, no reliance on others and no attachments; just allowing all things to take**

their course the whole day long, as though you were too ill to bother; unknown to the world; innocent of any urge to be known or unknown to others; with your minds like blocks of stone that mend no holes - then all the dharmas would penetrate your understanding through and through."

"Do not permit the events of your daily lives to bind you, but never withdraw yourselves from."

Joshu:

A monk asked, "I've heard that you have said, 'The Way is not acquired by practice, just don't become degenerate.' What is not being degenerate?" Joshu said, "Closely examining inside and outside." The monk said, "Then do you yourself closely examine or not?" Joshu said, "I closely examine." The monk said, "What fault do you have that you yourself closely examine?" Joshu said, "What is it that you have?"

Joshu said, "I can make one blade of grass be a sixteen-foot golden Buddha, and I can make a sixteen-foot golden Buddha be one blade of grass. Buddha is compulsive passions, compulsive passions are Buddha." A monk asked, "For the sake of whom does Buddha become compulsive passions?" Joshu said, "For the sake of all people Buddha becomes compulsive passions." The monk said, "How can they be escaped?" Joshu said, "What's the use of escaping?"

There you are! It's like a bible!

Tea

While I have you here I would like to say a few words about tea, rumored to be the drink of Zen Masters. I do not mean the sort of tea the English drink, that's ridiculous. I also do not mean those sad little bags of tea that are really just the dust of past leaves, served up to Westerners and often as not filled with flowers or something instead of tea dust. I mean tea! It's a leaf. You put it in some hot water and then later you drink it.

I have been drinking tea for some time now and I know as little about it as I did in the beginning, which says something for its merits. The sort of water, the sort of tea, the sort of pot, it can be confusing. I began drinking silver needle, then better silver needle, then really good silver needle, and then more or less anything with a whole tea leaf involved.

The tea related wisdom I pass on to you here is to drink it. Do not be distracted by the coffee consumers and their ilk who add milk and sugar to their beverages, invariably so they can drink milk and sugar and call it something. Do not be distracted by the many faux teas that are really just infusions of various plants that are better looked at than put in hot water. This is *tea* that I am talking about.

Sooner or later I will find someone that spent their lifetime understanding this plant as a beverage and they will explain it all to me if such a thing is possible. At that time I will of course let you all know what it is that I find out, if anything. None of it will have anything to do with *drinking* tea, I assure you. There is a double meaning in that, as Benedick once remarked, and no doubt he was right.

Interlude:

Ummon said, "A monk should know the eye of the ancient men. What was this eye?" Answering himself he said, "It is a toad dancing up to heaven."

6. Further Reading: Some old men

On the one hand people often become very angry when they are told that their religions are not Zen. The Buddhisms ferociously protect their identity which is ironic given the nebulous ground the word "Buddhism" stands on. Even more ironic is that those who are told that their religions are not Zen do not go off and read the old conversations by the Zen Masters. They assume they know all that is really essential to Zen. This is how we get into trouble in the first place, when we believe someone. Then, once we believe one person, believing someone contrary becomes very difficult. Even if "that's not what they said in their books" is the only new thing we are being asked to believe.

Mumonkan [A Bunch of Zen Masters]

The story goes that Mumon assembled a collection of koans called Mumonkan. Mumon means "Gateless", that was his monk-y name. "Kan" might mean the bar that keeps a door closed, or barrier, thus the title: Mumon's Barrier, or The Gateless Barrier. Sometimes it is referred to as The Barrier of the Way, the Gate of No, the Gateless Gate, or just the Gate.

Mumon compiled the Gateless Gate from the sayings of his favorite Zen Masters and other stuff. Then he wrote a single paragraph, sometimes a single sentence, as commentary. He also composed a single stanza for each Case. Not many Zen Masters wrote anything down themselves.

Some people refer to them as Cases, or koans, some say ko-an. Koan might be translated as "A case that holds something sharp." Really all they are is just pieces of conversations that people had with Zen Masters. Some stuff has been left out, like people asking where the bathroom is and demands for more tea.

Mumonkan is sort of the center of the history of the Zen conversation. There are a number of commentaries on Mumonkan, and of course R.H. Blyth, the incomparable Zen historian, produced the most thoroughly annotated Mumonkan anyone ever saw. It was the fourth volume of Blyth's *Zen and Zen Classics* series, but it often appears here and there as Mumonkan, by R.H. Blyth.

The Sayings of Joshu [Funny!]

Joshu is sort of the Robin Hood of Zen Masters, but the wise cracking version not the solemn war veteran version. This book is very short and mostly funny. The first few pages are a rather patronizing biography, but the rest is just Joshu being as silly as possible. Someone once asked me, "Why don't the monks see what's coming?"

This is an interesting book because there is so much material. Mumonkan is brief, that's part of its virtue, but you don't see the Masters being chased around by people demanding answers. To see into the traditional and cultural and historic context of these conversations requires a larger set of these exchanges, and Joshu's Sayings provides this.

The Zen Teachings of Huang Po: [Early Teaching]

Huang Po, aka Huang-po Hsi-yün, aka Huángbò Xīyùn, aka Ōbaku Kiun was a fourth generation student of the Sixth Patriarch of Zen. His teacher was Hyakujo, the fox koan Master. Huang Po's book is divided into chapters, some of them transcripts of lectures, some of them transcripts of dialogues between Huang Po and others.

Huang Po is yet another example of everything I've said here, funny, irreverent, offering nothing, teaching no dharma. You can't find a single useful thing or a single fault with him. In addition, like Joshu who comes a generation later from a different lineage, the extensiveness of Huang Po's record offers insights into the cultural and traditional questions and arguments of the time. Longer than Joshu, more lectures and less dialogue, but often Huang Po answers the very questions that people today who believe they know things are unable to answer.

The Third Patriarch's Faith in Mind

This is so short you wonder where he left the rest of it. Delightfully simple especially if you don't try to translate it yourself. Available on the internet in various translations, also it can be found in some books. D.T. Suzuki puts it in his *Manual of Zen Buddhism* which is mostly a survey of older texts.

Platform Sutra of the Sixth Patriarch

This is a long and uneven document with a wide array of different translations, maybe because as Suzuki says it was edited by followers of different time periods for political reasons, maybe because the Sixth Patriarch wasn't formally educated as were most of the monks of the time, who knows. The translation makes a big difference, so if you find one unintelligible try another. Suzuki has written extensively about it, especially in *The Zen Doctrine of No-Mind*, and there are excerpts from different versions floating around. Suzuki has some of it in *Manual of Zen Buddhism*. Most common is the 1930's translation, and if you compare it to Red Pine's translation you can see the complexity of the conversation.

Famous Buddhist Books that Aren't Zen

Anybody can write a book and put "Zen" in the title. Any religion can call their priests "Zen Masters". This is all just talk that will cause your eyebrows to fall out as the old men joked. If you talk about Zen then you must show some Zen or else you are no different than a priest in a temple who pretends that wooden Buddha statues are something more than wooden Buddha statues.

Dogen - *Shobogenzo*

A foundational text of those who call themselves Soto Zen Buddhists. As with the Bible, I haven't read this all the way through. Also like the Bible, I find there is room for skepticism. Anyone who discarded a Christian upbringing through intellectual effort will find similar sorts of efforts are necessary in sorting through Dogen's Shobogenzo.

People who read Dogen will often conclude they know something about Zen. People who read the old Masters will say little because they learned nothing. Dogen started his own religion, and these old Masters are nearly forgotten! This is the way it should be.

Shunryu Suzuki - *Zen Mind, Beginner's Mind*

Shunryu is not to be confused with D.T. Suzuki the noted Zen scholar. Shunryu is a Buddhist who says as much in his book, he says, he is "not a Zen Buddhist." Nobody pays any attention, or they take it for some sort of spiritual declaration, "We are all Buddhists". Shunryu is not a Zen Master, he is either a Buddhist Master or a Soto Buddhist Master, but not a Zen Master. He talks about having faith and his religious belief in Zazen meditation. Zen Masters don't have any faith, what would they want it for? Nevertheless, Dogen Buddhism's followers continue to call him a

71

Zen Master. He is widely beloved and respected for his wisdom and kindness.

Thich Nhat Hahn - *Peace is Every Step*

Thich is a Buddhist who writes about mindfulness. Mindfulness is not Zen. Also, a compassionate man. There is no such compassion in Zen. Thich's Wikipedia page mentions something about his early Zen training in meditation, I guess that's most of what there is to know. He is famous for many accomplishments and he has received great recognition for his political goals of peace and unity. These sorts of goals are not those of a Zen Master. Why would a Zen Master want peace and unity? People who want peace and unity should read Thich's books.

Brad Warner - *Hard Core Zen*

I haven't read the book! Feel free to send me an email about how Mr. Warner is able to explain that if you believe what he says, then you will believe him when he says Zazen meditation has something to do with Zen, rather than being just a religious form of meditation. *This is Revolution, remember.* "Take my word for it" is not a strategy we recognize. Don't take my word for it, read his book.

I have read blog entries about him, by him, in response to him. He seems a decent enough sort who enjoys a little of that righteous finger pointing that the religions are famous for. People who judge other people for their judginess or lack of true judiness are always entertaining. People who say "not Zen" are as bad as the rest, they are just not religious about it, and they are impartial in their sharing of their tea.

Judginess is not Dharma combat, Zen Masters didn't score Dharma combat, and there is no reason to start now. When I say "judgment" here, I mean dualistic thinking. When I say "dualistic thinking" I do not mean calling a staff a staff or refusing to admit that the rice is not the same as the bowl it comes in. The old men called this "telling night from day". Don't try to eat the bowl. That's probably not Zen. Dualistic thinking is saying that one bowl is kinder, gentler, more honest, or has more integrity than another bowl.

Remember in Zen there are no judges. There are Zen Masters and idiots, students and fools, and with no authority or hierarchy these are more or less all interchangeable. The various communities in the Buddhisms enjoy scandal or at least they like to read about it. I suppose it is because nobody is hitting them with a bamboo pipe and shouting "No!"

This is not to be confused with Soto Dogen Buddhism, where they hit people with sticks because of posture problems. You can't get into their Nirvana without good posture, or at least trying to have good posture, or at least recognizing that there is "good" posture.

Books of Zen Scholarship

Alan Watts - *The Way of Zen*

A philosopher who writes about Zen, or should I say an enormously popular and still comparatively honest philosopher who writes about Zen. He doesn't escape from the showmanship, but then he doesn't say he intends to at all. It is also interesting to note that his understanding evolves over the course of his life which is another tribute to his honesty. Not many people revisit their old conclusions, let alone their old works of nonfiction, and publicly declare their error. It is unlikely that I will, for example.

R.H. Blyth - *Mumonkan the Zen Masterpiece*, or *Zen and Zen Classics, Volume 4.*

The greatest Zen historian of the last fifteen hundred years, Blyth wrote four volumes on the history of Zen. You would think there was more history of Zen and there probably is. Blyth didn't have the internet. Our loss.

There are many other translations and commentaries on Mumonkan (other than Mumon's). I would have read them all prior to writing this book, but this book is so short that I didn't have time.

D.T. Suzuki - The Zen Doctrine of No-Mind.

I can't add anything to what he wrote. Suzuki's Buddhism is likely not the same as yours.

Some criticize Suzuki for supporting Japan's role in WW2. These claims are based on a few out of context quotations from one or two essays[48]. Further, the single often quoted book that makes these accusations about Suzuki, "Zen at War" was written by a Soto priest. When a member of a church casts aspersions on someone who criticizes that church, we should all proceed with more care than usual, not, as in this case, with less.

---

[48] http://www.thezensite.com/ZenEssays/CriticalZen/Suzuki_and-Question_of-War.pdf

Conclusion

Banzan said to the monks, "It is like a sword flung up into the sky. We can discuss whether it has reached there or not. There is no scar left on the sky, and the sword itself is not diminished."[49]

ewk
May, 2013

---

[49] p38 "Zen and Zen Classics, Volume 3 - R.H. Blyth - Google Books."
<http://books.google.com/books/about/Zen_and_Zen_classics.html?id=sgQYA
AAAIAAJ>

Made in the USA
Middletown, DE
04 December 2014